Stop!
In the Name of Love ...

... sang the 1960s cult band "The Supremes". The female trio, who represented and developed female views and voices unlike any other band in the 20th century, can most certainly be classified as one of the most successful bands in history. Their great success is largely ascribable to the wonderful Diana Ross, the lead figure of the band. And we are proud to say that we have a Diana of our own, to whom this book is dedicated. Even though our Diana is not the queen of Motown but rather the queen of plastic cameras, her achievements (i.e. photos) are equally tempting, feminine and charismatic. Furthermore, our Diana's mission is similar to that of The Supremes: exploring the female views and voices to the greatest extent! It is in the midst of their mission that we present "Dianalogues Part 1: Through a Woman's Lens".

Every so-called Dianalogue in this book explores and celebrates the great diversity of female perspectives. Whether these Dianalogues are created by women (as 26 of them are) or men (of which 2 brave individuals found their way in here) – they are provocative, philosophical, unexpected, funny and strong stories shot through a woman's lens: the Diana. Speaking of which, the cozy little word „Dianalogue" is made out of three parts: the word Diana (the camera), dialogue (like communication) and analogue (such as analogue photography). Complement these keywords with the community of approximately one million Lomographers worldwide and you pretty much know what Lomography is all about.

Yet, this project could only be realized in cooperation with our friends from colette*. The notorious Paris-based boutique and world-known trendsetter finely selected 10 women to contribute their images and words to this project. We from Lomography** complemented this excellent selection of highly interesting and creative female artists with 18 equally gifted Lomographers from our worldwide community. The outcome is 160 pages of pure positive discrimination coming from 28 artists from 12 countries and 4 continents! From Madeira to New York, Paris to Beijing, Los Angeles to Sydney to Berlin – our friends documented their adventures with their Diana, added their message and we slammed it all into this book.

When bringing all this together, we drew inspiration from Whoopi Goldberg (another great woman of our time) in "Sister Act 2". colette gave a shout out to her favourite sisters worldwide to join the "Through a Woman's Lens" gang, whereas we from Lomography held an online competition on www.lomography.com. The briefing was all the same for both: Select 10 of your finest images shot with a Diana camera, write a story, and send it to us. Just as mere singing, without that special something, wouldn't have cut it in Sister Mary Clarence's choir; the task here was not just to write captions to your images, but to create a unique storyboard of images and words, i.e.: a Dianalogue. Sometimes words need an image to fully express what we want to say – and sometimes an image needs some words to get to its full meaning. By combining the creative possibilities of these two forms of expression, a Dianalogue is a work of art on its own.

Now what is that camera called Diana really all about? This camera was originally built in China in the 1960s and is now being reproduced by Lomography as the Diana+. However its lo-fi techniques and plastic lens are surely not state-of-the-art technology (it wouldn't even have been 100 years ago), the images it creates have a certain dreamy atmosphere that makes it so special. As this camera serves you with only the very basic mechanics for producing a photo, a whole lot of creative possibilities are left open to you. You'll see for yourself in this book that the Diana, unlike any other camera we know, is a storyteller. You push down that shutter and what you and the Diana, especially its "woman's lens," saw, is now irrevocably burnt on film, saved for

eternity and materialized in the real world. Nobody can take this moment from you – yet nobody knows what this moment will look like when you get your prints back from the lab. Chance, distortions, and the knowledge that despite your best efforts you'll never really be able to guarantee the outcome – it's all these things that mark the path to what we call creative analogue photography.

Within the 160 pages of this book you'll see this path is full of surprises, excitement, experimentation, colours, blurs, rays of light, coincidences and endlessly different perspectives. What you'll find here is the finest (and first) selection of Dianalogues ever made. It was made from nothing more than 148 grams of plastic, a few rolls of film and 28 creative minds. If you are one of them, be sure to have our eternal love and gratitude for participating in this project! If you're not one of them, then give the Diana a shot, shoot through a woman's lens and pay us a visit at www.lomography.com. The next Dianalogue competition will be coming soon, and we'd be greatly pleased to welcome you there.

Long live Whoopi, Tina Turner and Diana Ross,

Your Lomographic Society International

* colette is famed for being one of the world's leading boutiques when it comes to groundbreaking products and trendsetting urban style, art and culture. Situated in rue Saint-honoré 213 in Paris' 1st district, colette is an institution not only in Paris but around the world. Pay them a visit offline or online at www.colette.fr

** The Lomographic Society International is a global organization developing and producing creative analogue photo cameras, accessories, books, fashion, satisfaction and more. We furthermore really believe that the future is analogue. Read more about us at the last pages of this book or on www.lomography.com.

The Diana F+
colette special edition

Its plastic lens, 2 shutter settings (daylight & "B"), 3 aperture settings, and manual focus are all hallmarks of the original Diana. On top of that, the Diana F+ offers a fully functioning flash, a removable lens and super-small aperture for pinhole images, two image formats (12 or 16 shots on a standard 120 roll), an endless panorama feature that allows for unlimited and nearly seamless panoramic shots, and both a standard tripod thread and shutter lock for easy shake-free long exposures. Uses all varieties of medium format 120 film.

Dating back to the early 1960s, the all-plastic Diana camera is a cult legend – famous for its dreamy, radiant, and lo-fi images. The Lomography Diana F+ is a faithful reproduction and a loving homage to the classic Diana – with a few new features tossed in.

Inspired by colette's unique style and design, the Diana F+ colette edition was conceived. Covered by colette's trademark blue spots it hosts all features of the Diana F+. The Diana F+ colette special edition, released in 2009, is exclusively sold at colette and www.lomography.com.

Dianalogues Part 1: Through a Woman's Lens

Girls with Guns

Pictures and Text by Jenny Mannerheim

"All you need for a movie is a girl and a gun."
Jean-Luc Godard

Leading ladies ...
Laetitia
Marion
Lauranne
Yan
Fanta
Marie
Calla

Shoot, Laetitia.

A real woman doesn't necessarily know what she wants.
Only thing she's really sure of is what she doesn't want; boredom, obligations and someone telling her how things are.

Shoot, Marion.

We see women with a tragedy hidden behind a casualness and carefree glamour. Women playing games. Women wearing trousers. Women complaining. Women behaving like kids. Women acting *masculin-feminin*. Women who believe their man can be salvaged by the birth of a child. Women as performers, and ... women as prostitutes.

All different but all the same.
Women being funny, clever, insightful, cruel and beautiful. Women expressing deeper themes and hiding darker notions.

They're loaded guns ready to pop off.
Chic or sick.
Joie de vivre with a sympathy for the devil.
Fresh and hypnotic.

Women looking for some fun, some affection and some love.
Women looking for a *raison d'être*, a reason to be true.

Shoot, Lauranne.

Take it or leave it.
Thinking of Godard and what he once said "You should feel about a woman, not a movie. You can't kiss a movie.".

Focusing on one woman at each time, giving her time, space and love, helping her show her deeper sides. He made us *FEEL* about women in his movies.

He shot women through a woman's lens, with a man's eye. Warning us about the fatality of our actions. Showing us that too much rebellion usually leads to a rupture. That love needs trust, not disgust. Making clear that any woman, if she's a real women, can turn any situation into a horror movie, as easily as she can turn it into a light-hearted farce ... with impeccable style.

Women who fear love.
Women who want to be taken care of.
Women crying.
Women wanting truth.
Women looking for reconciliation.

You need to feel a woman to understand her.

Shoot, Yan.

Men seem ridiculous. As if they were all freudian cowards still analyzing women from the angle of 'penis envy'*. You need to feel a woman to understand one. The eternal battle of the sexes. This eternal battle is probably what makes a woman such a caricature of herself. It's her ultimate frustration.

There is no way she can feel independant and strong, as long as she's not at ease with men, as long as she cannot be at ease with the man she loves.

Her use of *mise-en-scène* is what makes her doubt in her own authenticity. This is what brings her to her own insatisfaction and her *mépris*. A *mépris* that she ends up feeling for herself and for her lies. She knows no longer who she is. She is lost in her own plot. Feeling fake. Feeling misunderstood. Feeling that anyone who loves her must be an idiot. She'd would rather die than tell someone.

Pride and prejudice makes her own the downfall, leaving her with feelings of loneliness, emasculation and dissatisfaction. Bang Bang.

*Penis envy in Freudian psychoanalysis refers to the theorized reaction of a girl during her psychosexual development to the realization that she does not have a penis. Freud considered this realization a defining moment in the development of gender and sexual identity for women.

Shoot, Marie.

Escapism, distance.
Dreaming of being somewhere else with somebody else, of being someone else.
Fantasm-ing of a tempestuous relationship.

Shoot again.

Losing herself into her inner conflict and
her caracter changes.
Our girl is now a sad mix of B-movie
gangsters and childless mothers, a
doomed heroine, an ex-babysitter gone
bad ...
Her relationship is declining and she's
wanting to run away from herself.
She wants to depend on no one.
She is thinking of prostituting herself.
She is thinking of vivre sa vie.

Shoot, Fanta.

Staight forward elegance.
Understanding one's own feelings.
Reflection and self-examination.
Choosing what to share, what to keep
private.
Knowing how best to deal with one's
contentment or one's rage.
Listenening to others.

Shoot, Calla.

Time of Innocence.
Sleep. Food. Sex.
Not too much talking.
Tired of acting. Tired of playing a role.
A bout du souffle.
No more jealousy.
Women want real things in the end.
To feel real.
For their love to be real.
To put an end to the eternal battle of
the sexes.

10 DIMES

Pictures and Text by Feride Uslu

As a make up artist, I am usually expected to put my 'signature' on a model's face. Turn her into an 'uslu' beauty (whatever that may be; job by job, project by project, differences can be vast, but so what?) What might be identified as the picture's subject, the face and perhaps its human tale, is transformated down to mere canvas. In the end, the signature visible to the all is a brand name. That same name that signed the check. The relation to the face is hardly of any consequence, aside from a few celebrity brands, it is totally interchangeable in that regard. My project for Lomo turns this concept on its head. It brings that which is dear to me, the very core of a subject, to the surface. I mean the woman, the individual. She has a name because she needs one to discriminate. She has a story to tell. All of the women in my Lomo-project have very strong eyes, and all but one have an "i" in their name, which, though NOT intended, I find it worth mentioning): Bianca, Camilla, Juliane, Ingrid, Niki, Karin, Maren, Katharina, Rike and myself. Focusing on a woman's eye has been natural to me since my childhood. I grew up in an Islamic environment. The headscarves on the pictures originate in that very same environment, most are hand crafted in my Turkish home village

from where they go all over the world to the global fashion centres ... my pictured girlfriends wrapped them very casually, as if they were just going out to the cotton fields. All of the key 'ingredients' have been topped up by putting each woman's genuine signature on their face. She is her own author and any good author signs her own work! It is a nearly impossible task for the artist herself to sign on her own face (just try it!), we created stencils from the handwritings so I could airbrush the signature. Besides being the photographer and the creator here, in a way, this also makes me the counterfeiter.

48 Hours in Madeira
with Diana and I

Pictures and Text by Tommy

26 June, Thursday
12:20 p.m.
I tilted my head and took a deep breath. The air certainly felt more refreshing than the London I had left behind.
It might seem random that I am in Madeira, even for a short stretch. My curiosity was piqued after Funchal* appeared on my blog visitor's map, courtesy of Google Analytics. It coincided with a sudden interest in the provenance of Madeira cake, an English supermarket shelf standard. With a little context provided by Wikitravel, my holiday destination was picked. So, slightly more thought went into this trip than merely throwing darts at a world map.

12:55 p.m.
After the inevitable humdrum of travelling (passport control, anticipating our luggage to appear on the conveyor belt), we hopped into a rented car from Avis and off we went to embrace sweet freedom, if only for two days ...

1:11 p.m.
Instead of heading to our base in Funchal, we drove towards the village of Santo da Serra for a quick lunch. I had flirted with the romantic idea of spontaneous exploration: arriving in a foreign land with nothing but my Diana and discovering as I went along. Since Madeira is a rather compact 741 km² and with a bit of a reputation as an OAP paradise**, it just might be the perfect location for a non-thrill-seeking adventurer like me. In the end, my fastidious nature won. In my Moleskine rests more than 10 pages of research: I already had a rough idea of places I'll be visiting, food I'll be eating and even things I'll be buying.

1:44 p.m.
Lunch was at A Nossa Aldeia, a place known for its rustic charm and "locals for customers". Other than a table to my right, I saw plenty of my kind around this family-friendly place. I guess everyone had read the same Cadogan Guides. I chose the "Aldeia Special", and was ambushed by a heaving plate of grilled steak topped with a fried egg and accompanied by frankfurters, fried maize cubes and a few token salad greens. A basic and homey meal enhanced by the crotchet lace-edged tablecloths and floral-tiled walls.

2:44 p.m.
Next stop, Camacha, famed for its wicker basket industry. The road was extremely steep but locals had no problem speeding past us. Have I mentioned how mountainous Madeira is? At one point during our ascent, we were above cloud level. I wondered what it would be like to live in houses on the terraced slopes and be greeted by clouds in your face every morning.

3:09 p.m.
Arrived at O Relógio, the village square. The climate on the island varies with the altitude and here in Camacha it is definitely tropical. The thermometer in the car registered 31°C.

3:23 p.m.
Into the shop where baskets, trays, chairs, tables, animal head trophies*** and all sorts of wicker-ware can be found. In an act of incredible self-restraint, I chose to take home only one picnic basket.

3:58 p.m.
Check-in time at Funchal, so southwards we went. A careless turn took us down a one-way street with a dead end. We escaped, but the car suffered slight scratches to the window mirror and bumper. Road – 1: Us – 0.

5:14 p.m.
Settled in at Funchal Design Hotel, so it was time to head out again. I visited the nearby Bio-Logos. Visiting the local organic food store has become a travel ritual for me.

6:18 p.m.
Wandering around the main shopping district, I gasped when I caught sight of the blue signboard of Fabrica Sto. Antonio. Even before I stepped into the shop, I could see that everything was perfect – at least for me. This traditional bakery is full of handmade cakes, biscuits, sweets and jams, and of course, a friendly uncle eager to promote their goods. I picked up a pack of charmingly wonky Marie biscuits and banana jam, just the things for reliving this trip when back home in London.

8:15 p.m.
After a promenade by the seafront, it was dinnertime at the dependable O Jango in the Old Town. Walking down Rua de Santa Maria we saw another side of Funchal – the derelict and the abandoned.

8:53 p.m.
The starter is the addictive bolo do caco: a crispy, chewy flatbread warmed and smothered with garlic herb butter. I also got acquainted with another island specialty, espada (black scabbard fish) topped with fried bananas.

10:05 p.m.
Walking back to the hotel, we passed Golden Gate Café, an 1841 hangout which boastfully claims to be one of the "corners of the world". I could only spot a lone pair of men sitting at a table with playing cards. Well, it is Thursday …

27 June, Friday

7:11 a.m.
Reviewed my route for the day. My original, ambitious plan involved going across the mountains to Santana for triangular thatched houses, followed by a hike to Queimadas forest park. Then would be back to the southern tip again before heading west along the coastline. After yesterday's taster of the steep terrain, I sensibly scrapped my plans and weighed going North or heading West.

8:50 a.m.
But first, Mercado dos Lavradores, the farmers' market. The fish section seems to be where all the action is at: Giant Blue Marlin were cut up with knives that were equally as giant, the notoriously ugly black scabbard fish were being scrubbed for sale, and boxes of fresh caught mackerel sat waiting to be picked. Elsewhere I was overwhelmed by a rainbow selection of fresh produce – yellow bananas and potatoes, red tomatoes and peaches, pink cherries and borlotti beans, green lettuce, cabbages and various other unidentifiable vegetables.

11:18 a.m.
We go West! A seemingly endless curvy and uphill road takes us to the mountainside village of Estreito do Camara de Lobos.

12:17 p.m.
After a crazy, mind twisting drive, we finally arrive at the thoroughly modern Estreito do Camara de Lobos. It is busy compared to the sleepy villages I've visited. Our reward was lunch at Restaurante Santo Antonio, where the best beef espetada is said to be found. Cubes of herb-rubbed beef are grilled before being hung at each table on a foot-long skewer.

1:56 p.m.
Calheta has the atmosphere of a happy seaside resort with its man-made sandy beach helped out by massive cement cubes. Sunbathing however, was not our aim here.

2:24 p.m.
We are slightly disappointed but hardly surprised to learn that Madeira cake does not actually come from this island and is likely to be a British invention. Nonetheless there is bolo de mel, a dense cake flavored with sugar cane molasses and studded with nuts. A tip-off said that Engenhos da Calheta, an old sugar cane rum distillery, was the best place to get them.

2:36 p.m.
The sound made by the advance wheel on the Diana has got a lizard all excited. The more I turned, the nearer it came. I hurriedly reloaded my film while hoping that the impassioned lizard would not leap onto my lap.****

3:09 p.m.
Perched on top of a craggy cliff, the modern lines of art gallery, Centro das Artes da Calheta, looked strangely at home with the raw landscape. We might not be able to have a bird's eye view of the island, but being on top of this building came close.

3:37 p.m.
After the high comes the low. We were down on the ground once again, this time at the pretty seaside village of Jardim Do Mar. A tropical fruit ice-cream break was followed by a little nosing around the banana plantations and vegetable plots.

7:14 p.m.
Back in Funchal Old Town for dinner as we were too tired to consider any viable alternatives. Ended up in Arsenio's, a straight up, unapologetic tourist trap. Dinner was less than satisfactory but at least there was comforting bolo do caco.

28 June, Saturday
9:36 a.m.
Back on the road again for the easy drive
to the airport. I realized there is still so
much to see – I haven't even been to
any gardens for the famed blooms of
the island.

10:44 a.m.
The queue at the check-in counter was
snaking. We decided to take it easy at
the airport café. An opportunity to try
some Portuguese snacks before we go.
Pretty decent for airport fare and my
favorite was pasteis de bacalhau, a fritter
filled with flaked salt cod.

12:20 p.m.
On board Easyjet 3264, London in about
three hours. The plane has yet to leave
the runway but I'm already planning my
return.

*Funchal is the capital of Madeira Island

**Madeira is said to be a British Old Age Pensioners'
    preferred holiday destination due to its year-round
    sub-tropical weather, lack of noisy party destina-
    tions and a ridiculously diverse range of trees and
    flowers.

***Woven, not hunted!

****After frogs, lizards rank next on my most terrifying
    animal list

One Two, One Two ...

Pictures and Text by Fafi

My experience with the Diana is quite possibly the worst experience I have ever had with photography, an art that I studied since I was 15 years old. I began with my father's Bessamatic Voïgtlander or sometimes used his cool little spy Minox. I would develop my own film and prints. I always had a nagging suspicion that my father led a double life. In one life, he was the loving family man, the other, an agent with the U.S.

government, or maybe the Russians. I had these thoughts because he would travel for his job at "La Dépêche du Midi" the local newspaper in my hometown of Toulouse. Sometimes he worked till midnight. I could honestly say that I was the only one at school who had a father working that late into the night. The entire summer I spent in the company of that turquoise camera. We went to Corsica, to Portugal, to the Fuji Rock

festival in Japan. We spent two months in New York – I had her forever held tightly to my neck taking what I thought were "abfab" pictures with her! I was really looking forward to finally seeing those pics, especially because it is really, really difficult to hang out (drunk) at a music festival with a camera this big, while grabbing the backstage atmosphere.

Now, she is a very light camera and a door opener because everyone wants to talk with the girl with the cute blue camera. I was on top of the world.
So, you can imagine how I looked and felt when the LOMO team sent me my 10 cans of pics ... all black.

I took my cute and ungrateful Diana and put her in a box, to the left, to the left. We were still in New York when this tragedy unfolded, and honestly, I didn't have any energy to get back into it. After all the trips we went on, and the friends we met together, my Diana gave me black, empty pictures.
Our great love affair was over!
I turned my back on the project.

The Paris team joined the New York team to ask me to get back in the game, they told me they knew what the problem was, they gave me another one, and also gave me 3 days past the deadline. So here's what we found in Paris, Diana and her jilted lover, delicately trying to rebuild a broken trust.

My Mini
Wall of China

Pictures and Text by Sophie Toporkoff

"Do you have a valid passport?"
"Uh, yeah sure *(who does she think I am?)*.
Why do you want to know?"
"You leave tomorrow for Beijing. We just
need to get you a super rush visa, and
then you're off."

That's how my 36 hours in China began.
My name is Sophie, I'm the Communica-
tions Art Director of the Maison Martin
Margiela. It seems that Sam, our PR

person, has no one else she can send at the last minute to give press interviews for the upcoming Maison exhibition in Beijing ... at the same time, I was the curator of the show, so it sort of makes sense that I'm the one going.

10-hour flight

What's a spokesperson supposed to do again? Well, I've got about ten hours to crack the thousand and one secrets of the Maison. I cram through all the literature while asking myself one fundamental question: Was it really such a good idea to go to Art School and to find myself, fifteen years later, on a plane headed for Beijing, studying up like I was taking a High School physics exam? I stop freaking out and test myself. Line 4? Wardrobe for women. Line 11? Accessories for men and women. A tough one: Line 13? Objects and publications. Launch date of the Men's Collection? Uhh ... Spring/Summer 99? I can't help dozing off.

The Dream

Arrival. Check-in at The Westin (sounds like a good film title ...). "Chinese Fusion Food" lunch. Store visit. Press conference. One-on-one interviews. It's raining. Opening of the show. Peking duck dinner.

Sleep. Meetings all morning. I've done my duty.

Six hours! I've got six full hours before my plane takes off ... a dream. I didn't expect all this time, all this ... FREEDOM! I hadn't hired a tour guide, hadn't checked anything on the internet, didn't ask my friends what to do ... so what should I do? I think of the first three clichés that come to mind with the word "Beijing". Should I go eat noodles? That's lame. A guided tour of the Olympic Stadium? I'm not gonna join the propaganda machine. The Forbidden City? They say it closes at 3pm. Eureka! The Great Wall of China, of course! I head to the hotel information desk. They call me a taxi, and in a second I'm on the highway, navigating a mess of cars, passing by the big new stadium (guess it was fated ...), surrounded by buildings under construction every which way – all of this in between a few remaining pagodas and a heavy fog settling in along the sides of the road as we head farther and farther away from the capital.

The Reality

"We've arrived. I'll wait for you here." At least I think that's what my driver tells me. Where's the entrance? The fog is so thick that I can hardly see my feet. I follow the other tourists, all of them Chinese (is every

Westerner boycotting China or what?) When I get there, they throw me onto a sort of gondola ski lift which I haven't seen since I went skiing at the 2-Alpes in 1994 – and I'm telling myself that this really wasn't my idea of how one should visit the Great Wall, that I should be walking or even running across it, like an emperor from the Qing dynasty. But here I am on the lift. It's modern, I guess. But I'm pretty sure the wall looks better on foot.

And what's all that white stuff everywhere? The fog has invaded everything, and I can't see ANYTHING!! I'm alone in this ridiculous lift, half-laughing and half-crying, and I can't believe that this wall, which they say can be seen from space – and surely from the naked eye – is for me, who's riding just above it, completely invisible.

Ah, look, the lift is landing. Contrary to my fears, we didn't do a round trip but actually landed on the Great Wall itself. Anyway that's what they call it. According to the brochure, it's 6,700 kilometers long. If I go by my eyesight, it's about … two meters long. I plunge into the white which surrounds me. And then, it starts to rain. I try to adapt the most positive attitude possible, and wind up persuading myself that it's not the Great but the Little Wall of China that I've come to see. And in fact, it's actually quite cute.

欢迎
您再来
PLEASE COME AGAIN.

Ladies of
the Night

Pictures and Text by Claw Money

In my dream world, I would just be around women. Not that I do not love men, as I do. I am not a lesbian but I fully support the gay movement! I love women and want to help them and I want them to help me. Sometimes I am disappointed by them and want them to be better – tougher, smarter, and more powerful and less caught up in the trappings of so-called femininity. There should be more women in the work place, and making the same money as their male associates. Judge them on their character and wits, not their looks and outfits. I love beauty and God knows I love fashion, but I think as far as women go, it is a little too surface and we need to instill much more value to more important characteristics of what a woman should be.

Armed with my 'DIANA LOMO', I went to the work that day, to my all female staffed office, hoping to finish up this project. It was already late because of numerous reasons. The number one was being over booked with projects and work! So I told my ladies – "SMILE! This is for colette!" And snapped them look-ing rather annoyed – after all they have a lot of work to do as well. The phone was ringing off the hook with requests. We were going crazy filing orders, finishing up the design for the line and the lookbook. This was already late by 2 weeks! Spring is a hard season for us to design because we are all feeling dark and broody usually this time of year. Spring is the time where Mother Earth becomes fertile again and you want to skip through the fields, but we were not in this head space. We were focused on projects and my project was DIANA! Smile girls, NOW! Cat, my smart and serious administrator was not amused. I was holding her up from the mounds of work ahead of her. I would not let her say no. Snap. Then Haley my ingeniously creative right hand wo-man, was giving me the hurry up look. She was hung over and not feeling her best. Snappy snap! Hannah, my astute all around executor gave me one of her dazzling smiles. Snap! Got them all. Now we can all get down to our tasks at hand. I put the camera down and went in front of my computer.

After a 10 hour day in the virtual trenches, I went off into the night. I was to have an evening celebrating WOMEN! First, a dinner to announce a new wom-en's product from the famous French brand, Lacoste. Then, off to the 15 year anniversary soiree for the modern femi-nist publication, BUST MAGAZINE! Yay WOMEN! Celebrate us in all our glory. In keeping in the tradition of the DIANA, I was out to hunt these lovely creatures down. Capture them just for an instance.

My first stop was to meet one of my very best girlfriends. The beautiful, wonderful, and talented Danielle Levitt – famed photographer and girl about town. She was my date for the night; my husband was not invited nor did he even want to attend. Lucky me, I was at her place drinking wine, then off we went to Rice for our Lacoste dinner hosted by Pam Bristow and Matt Goias – whom I both adore. Their invite literally said "As you know, our client Lacoste is the originator of the tennis (or polo) shirt which completely revolutionized athletic and casual clothing almost eighty years ago. This fall, Lacoste is launching their totally redesigned women's polo, the PF170. So we decided to gather some of our favorite NYC girls (and their boys) and give them a taste of the new Lacoste staple.

When we arrive the dinner party is already in full swing, of course we are little late. The guest list is a very downtown mix. The fabulous filmmaker Jauresti Saizarbitoria looking awesome, cute as button and blogger extraordinaire Wendy Lam of Nitrolicious.com, photographer Angela Boatwright (who is one of my favorites), bloggers Jennifer and Gaby from WorshipWorthy.com and Claudia from 'Me' magazine, just to name a few! There were some notable dudes there too, but who cares! This story is only about the girls.

We ate soy meatballs (I recently found out soy is not good for women, it makes you infertile), chicken curry and delicious grilled vegetables. We drank some rum concoction; I was getting a bit tipsy. I have a very low tolerance to alcohol, 2 drinks and I am buzzing and after 3, I am drunk. I was drunk! I was anticipating the dessert course and then my lovely date in pink chiffon (Danielle usually only wears black) informed me that we were late to the BUST party ... and it was going to be mobbed.

I thank my hosts and kiss my friends, then run out to Houston St. to get a cab. Danielle is wearing sky high shoes so she trails slowly, even though she insisted that we leave in a hurry. We laugh and talk about the people at the dinner – about how good it is to see Matt Goias because she hasn't seen him in years! I actually met Matt at Danielle's house Christmas in 2003. He said "I have a tattoo from your ex-boyfriend!" and believe it or not, that is a rare thing. I also have a tattoo from my ex-boyfriend, but the ex only did a few tattoos and only for a short time – we are in the ex-boyfriend tattoo club! Whatever! As it turns out Matt and I have much more in common than just that. Anyhow, we are driving to this big fête at a locale by Pier 17, Spiegelworld.

I have not been partying much for the last few years. It is not as much fun as it used to be; the people are blander than in years past and I am getting old. I like to fancy that I have been all over this great city, know all venues, and have a handle of what goes on in nightlife, though I do not really participate in it anymore. I do not know nor did I ever hear of this destination. We arrived a few doors down from the smelly fish market. It was raining and seemingly abandoned. I asked Danielle "Where the hell are we going?" She said "To the BUST party, silly, and we are late!"

BUST, or Bust magazine, I know very well. I am a contributor to this publication. I am a fan of these girls since the beginning! I remember when I was a bartender at the infamous "No-Tell" bar on Avenue A in the early 90's, they would come in and drop off their photo-copied fanzine and paper stickers. Who knew they would be a real deal mag? ME, that's who! I watched them grow from East Village zine to 5th Avenue glossy. They are the voice of the modern feminist, one who sews and cooks because she wants to! I often ponder modern feminism and wonder why it is so "craft fair"? Why are these 21st Century girls knitting, quilting, and needlepointing? They do it because they want to! The "Do It Yourself" or "DIY" mantra started in these very pages – and now it is its own culture! Bust pioneered this new wave of crafty bitches (and

I use the word "bitches" in the most loving and respectful way) and put them in front of the other like-minded girls who were reading the only American magazine for women not dominated by fashion or recipes. This magazine had big BALLS – and a big BUST!

So back to Spiegelworld, it was literally a circus tent from the 1920's on a downtown pier overlooking the East River. Lucky for us it has stopped raining and we were on the VIP list, so it was a painless entrance. Once inside there were go-go dancers, drag kings, Amy Sedaris was hosting, and we were awaiting a performance from Leslie and the LY's. This band (or are they performance art?) is really all Leslie Hall of Gem Sweater (google it).

She gained fame and popularity from Vice magazine's (when they were in top form) feature about her and her vast collection of genius and terribly tacky sweaters, that she documented by taking self portraits in. She fast became an internet sensation and with this new notoriety started a band, which she is the enthusiastic lead singer of. I hope she can live up to all the hype.

Danielle and I enter the stage area and there are people on 6-foot stilts. Lots of chicks in the audience, but none that I recognize from my East Village days, when BUST was a newbie and we were all swilling beer and complaining about dudes. This was a new age of readers and fans. Lots of them! Soccer mom types, dykes, glamour girls and plain janes. There were also tons of men there! Granted mostly a gay male crowd, the friends of the feminists! I briefly saw Laurie and Debbie, the co-founders of the mag, kissed them and said hello. But they were off again running around like crazy loons because this was their gig. Where were my people? My homegirls? Granted most of the girls I ran with, that used to pump their fists in the air are now pumping breast milk for their baby's lunch. Did we all give up the wild times for motherhood? Is that the destination for young feminists? Crafting and motherhood?

A tear came to my eye thinking of days gone by when we had all-girl bowling nights on University Pl., at that now chic bowling alley when it was cheap and dirty. When we would go on all-girl business trips to Vegas and Barcelona and have 4 or 5 girls to a room. Of course, all the boys wanted to hang with us. When we would all go up to the woods and run around naked in the night, drinking ridiculous amounts of alcohol and enjoying the freedom of being around close friends. Girlfriends! Best friends! Now I am married. Mind you, to the most wonderful man. We have a dog, 2 cats, a house and a car. We keep talking about getting pregnant. Who am I?? Will I one day start knitting just for the fuck of it? I already sew, so I am half way there. How I wish I could go back in time, to be a careless young, bon vivant with boundless energy doing all the things bad girls do...

Leslie and the LY's hit the stage and my pondering and reminiscing stopped. If I thought her gem sweaters were good, I was super impressed by her gold fringed spandex jumpsuit and her early 80's Gloria Vanderbilt eyeglasses; her signature eyewear style. What they lacked in musical originality and talent they far made up for in energy and good plain old fashioned fun. One song, I would almost say was a banger! Leslie, whose look is usually resembling an elderly 3rd grade teacher, looked Rubenesquely sexy and completely free of self doubt and insecurity! This is a beautiful woman, though not the societal norm. She is a true babe! And she knows it! And shows it! Not afraid to be who she is, even if it is taking the piss out of rock and roll. I ran to the front with my LOMO and had to capture images of this woman; this energy and vitality. Her bandmates were super cute but my eyes were transfixed on the gold suited singer jumping around the stage, like a super hero.

Next came the world famous *BOB*, finally an old friend! *BOB* may be the only person in the world to legally have changed her name with asterisks in the spelling. She and her big, bad self did what a *BOB* does; an old fashioned striptease and a flash of her famous, very ample bosoms. I was unable to take any photos as I had finished all the frames in the camera and was stuck in the stage area, away from my purse filled with rolls of film. So I cheered instead! Yay *BOB*! We met years ago in a vintage store where we were both friends with the owner. Good times!

As I turned to head back to the banquet where my homies (all boys but Danielle!) were holding my handbag, the Pontani sisters, another burlesque phenom-enon – 3 stripping sisters from New Jersey, each one different with unique talents, hit the stage.
Now I am completely caught up in a sea of fans and cannot get back to re-load my LOMO. Bitches! Get off me! On second thought, I decide to be cool and just watch the show. The first of the girls is fun and not overtly sexual. She is all smiles and has a vintage costume, mostly sequins and satin. A fan dance begins and it is sweet. Very tame compared to today's porno standards and strip club floor shows. The next sister (yes, they are really sisters!) is a bit of the same; flirty and cheeky. Her costume and smile are not as vibrant as her other sister, who performed first. Next is the 3rd sister, who looks nothing like the other two. She is tall and blonde, with large, droopy eyes and a huge mouth. The other girls were dark, short and tiny. Sexy Italian girls you would expect to see chewing gum loudly at a Mets game. This one was dressed in a sultry sailor outfit. She started off innocent enough and then by the end of her show, was shoving her whole fist in her mouth. Impressive! Scary! Feminist? Maybe. I was a bit confused by the self mouth fisting, but who am I to say the rest of ladies don't like that? Now I knew I had to head back to get my stuff and more film.

It was very dark in the tent and I was drunk. I loaded roll after roll, but could not get the camera to work! Turn on the lights! Bring back the girls! I kept giving the camera to Danielle, who is a profes-sional. Make it work! We peeled the plastic packages off rolls and rolls of film, trying to fit them correctly into DIANA, who was not cooperating! Danielle, being such a great friend tried steadfastly, fending off hellos and kisses to really try to load this baby properly. I was grateful, but do not think I got another decent shot for the rest of the night!

Now with DIANA, safely tucked in my bag I was defeated! I have pictures to take. With digital machines I have gotten spoiled. You can take so many photos and edit on the spot. But this camera was different. What was inside of my DIANA? A story of women? The tale of my 24 hours photo hunt? You tell me.

Hard to be a Woman Nowadays

Pictures and Text by Helena Ichbiah

Hard to be a woman nowadays
A woman, a mother, a worker, a wife, a mistress, a bitch, an icon, so much ... Sometimes you just forget to be some of these, and you begin to be just one, sometimes you forget to live, to do all you have to do.
Sometimes you wish to

fly in the air, like you don't care

have fun with marins like in a movie

be "une belle plante" means you're just
beautiful next to your man, nothing else

to go on a road movie, leave everything
behind

even be a cowboy, and just follow the
rails

be a child again, have a nice yellow
inflatable duckie ring to protect you

have the time for nothing

play sucker with the teenagers next door

enjoy having a big shadow

and for an end, a Japanese suicide in Paris.

Lola's Journey

Pictures and Text by Daphné Bürki

The doors of Bretagne open to Lola and her procession, as she journeys to the Atlantic Ocean with her little universe in tow.

She has come all this way on her own two feet, crossing great plains and wandering through the many green parks in between. Her dreams are brightly coloured. The music she listens to comes from Texas, or maybe it's the North of Canada, I can never really remember. It was her grandparents, the ones who crossed the Urals themselves, who taught her the language of the great outdoors.

But who is Lola?

She is the girl of the century, whose visions are so mixed-up with the images of our time that she had to recreate them, restore and deliver them to us.

Along with a compendium by Louise Labé, Lola's uncle left her a Lomo, a little sky-colored plastic camera. He then gave the following instructions:
    Go, child, run, sleep, dream, love, never stop until you have something to show of your experiences and tell us of the happiness you've found.

From then on, Lola has followed her instinct, comparing what she sees through her eyes, with the apparitions in the photos she takes. In these visions she pictures herself as a baby, in the arms of her parents, then as woman, then an animal, then the sun, the sea. Each photo is an exact reproduction of the images in her mind.

Her suitcase has just about enough space to fit her little blue camera and a record player, on which she can play her music.

Her mother tells us:
    From the very first photos, it was incredible; in that little camera, Lola had found the eye that sees the world her way.

Through the lens of that blue Lomo, she catches her parents, her uncle; she can see the sea – the whole world! It never leaves her side.

Colours melt under the sun. Forms become faint in substance; 'grain upon grain' her uncle Hamm would say, and Lola would recall the verses of Louise Labé, as she walks on the beach, reciting them to black-feathered cormorants, while she searches for sea shells in the sand.

At one point, a girl, about Lola's age, approaches her, wistfully soliloquising, asking questions that want no reply:
    What are you doing with your life?
The girl's name was Marie.

    Why act as if it's already over? I'm leaving now, but ...

She stops suddenly and stares aghast at the photo Lola is holding up to her. In it she recognises herself, ten years from now.
    Where did you find this? She asks.
    I mean when?
    When and where?

I don't know, Lola replied, it's just my way of seeing the world.

Bright colours sparkle brighter.

All textures, ephemeral, expand into nothingness.

Meanwhile, Lola's father is resting back at camp. His daughter's photos have shown him the colours of the rainbow.

We can see her father's presence in all of Lola's pictures. It is he who emanates the strong odours, like a jennet trudging along the sidewalks. The rolling expanse of the world's parks, that, by now Lola knows back to front, was planted by her father's own brawny hands.

Placed side by side, Lola's pictures tell us a story, the story of a young girl, moved by the beauty of the world before her eyes.

Fields are now considerably wider.

For twenty years Lola's mother has encouraged Lola's love for the stars.

Lola and her mother are thankful that the days of unhealthy aestheticism are over, and through it all, they've managed to maintain their fellow traveler's trust. They've undoubtedly been enriched by this journey.

Lola's mother gathers energy from the beauty of flowers, and it is she who taught her daughter to respect the colour scheme of empty forms.

Lola, her father and her mother are all present in Lola's pictures.

A Farandole of grains. With volumes and wraiths, photography becomes chemistry, perfume.

Lola's uncle Hamm is a dignified old hippopotamus of a man, who gave Lola the Lomo of her dreams.

That's why film photography irritated the incredulous Marie, according to Louise, Lola's poet and now friend.
Wasn't she the girl who saw herself pictured ten years from now?

Clic, clic! The flash goes off, the speed of lightning, giving the darkness a terrible fright; the mechanism then reloads and superimposes two distinct images. It's called Palimpsest photography!

Everyone appears in Lola's visions.

These *visions* are gentle; full of subtle perfumes. A mixture of fresh mountain dew and the hot vapours of the sea.

Look! The sunrise gives it an explosion of texture!

These are murmurs Lola hears from the torrent of vivid recollections constituting every step of her epic journey.

Where do the pixels come from?

Where does one's gaze fall?

Ecce Lomo.

Another night arrives at vanishing ambers of daylight. The family set-up camp for the night and will set off again in the morning. Sunglasses on the double, ready to dictate the next shot. Bretagne has opened its doors to Lola.

Every one of Lola's *visions* is a dream encapsulated on the printed photograph taken from the Lomo's camera angle.

In the middle of the night, a flash lights up the bay. Lola is dreaming and from where she stands, she has caught a glimpse of the whole world.

57

(6)

(9)

(10)

HELLS BELLS

Pictures and Text by Linlee Allen

In a plethora of ways I believe women are already given a heads up being born under the golden chromosome. And the best part of it all is awakening so many different parts of our personalities (read: the goddess within) pending on the city in which you live.

I'm Linlee. I was raised in Australia. On my 21st birthday I embarked upon an adventure which ushered me to a place called Paris, which is where I believe I truly found my spirit not to mention enduring the transformation from girl to woman. Although you truly never lose that inner girl. Especially if you consider yourself utterly boy crazy like me. I love boys. I love the ways of seduction and the discoveries and the liberation you can feel from different experiences with different members of the opposite sex. I appreciate the dichonomy between what you dream and what you create. Its about Quantum Physics: you think it, you bring it home. On a poignant full moon in 2007 I created a wish list for a guy. Two weeks later I found him whilst researching an article I was working on for a magazine. Long story short, he lived in Los Angeles. He came to Paris, we attempted a long distance relationship for a while and then, several months later, I transplanted myself to America. And so the tale of this adventure begins ...

Some people come to Hollywood to become stars. Sometimes late at night if you're up in the hills you can even see a few for yourself. I'm talking about the ones on the screen not in the sky. Once I saw David Lynch driving along Mulholland Drive. And legend has it that the ghost of Orson Welles can be seen in the coffee shop where he used to frequent on a nightly basis. Its called Sweet Lady Jane. Not far from where he lived in a suburb called Brentwood is where I arrived. A stone's throw from the 70's style apartment block which I called home was the place where Marilyn Monroe killed herself. Fifty years later her death is still a mystery. Everyone wanted what she had. Not me. Although I did like the fact that she hooked up with Arthur Miller. I'm more into Maria Callas myself.

Much can be said about relationship break-ups. For use of a better expression: they suck. But they bring you to a new place, both spiritually and physically. You drop weight. You revert to being a girl again. You cry. You listen to advice from friends. And then you move on. I found a total gem of a place in Beverly Hills which serves me quite nicely thank you. Never in a million years did I ever imagine I would be living in 90210. But I do now. That's my place there in the picture. I live below two dyke's who have super loud sex once a month and play lots of Missy Elliott full blast to try and hide their shrieks of pleasure. I don't know what they're doing up there but its working for them. I took this photo from my front garden during an earthquake that happened recently. They happen fairly frequently in California.

Cars turn me off. Bikes turn me on. Boys on bikes turn me on. Bigtime. They're in control. They know where they're going and they're having fun on the way to their destination. Flying in the wind. That's my style. What's always good is turning the negative of a red light into a positive by witnessing some street art posted beside the precise place where you're motionless.

I haven't been in America long enough to call it home, but I appreciate the irony of settling in a place ruled by three colors: Red, White and Blue. Which is kinda ironic considering I was raised in Australia (red, white and blue, hello?) and from there lived in France (tri-color love once more). In this land of stars and stripes people watch too much television. They believe in a strange world filled with cliche's and money and 99 cent stores.

The West is best. I believe it. Los Angeles is a strange place filled with iconic objects like palm tree's, for example. Whoever thought of planting thousands of palm tree's all those years ago must surely be rewarded with some sort of shrine in heaven. And what about the weather? Sunshine gives maxi-amounts of vitamin D which is the essence of all things good. It's impossible not to be at your best in the West. Anais Nin

decamped to California many years ago. Even Tamara De Lempicka made the move from Paris to Beverly Hills. They called her the Baroness with a paintbrush. I don't know what they call me but I'll bet you fifty bucks the pool boys at the Beverly Hills Hotel are starting to get suspicious every time I insist on paying for iced coffees with cash instead of giving them my room number to start up a tab. Posing as a hotel guest is not a crime.

My friend Laura found a dog on the highway at Silverlake one day on her way to work. No collar, no nothing. This dog was on its last legs and to say that she was knocking on death's door would be an accurate presumption. Rescue dogs are a dime a dozen around these parts. I called her "Luckydog." Six months later we're best buddies. Sometimes I wake up in the middle of the night and she is lying next to me in bed with her head on the pillow. My friend Jen tells me dogs are great for slutty tendencies too. "You bring the guy back home and then you think to yourself, well, he could stay but that's taking up the dog's position on the bed and are they really worth it?" Jen knows best.

The World Needs a
Charismatic Dictator
(and other short stories)

Pictures and Text by Shauna T

The world needs a charismatic dictator. And it would help if they were photogenic.

Stalin offered an actor a job. It was the job of a lifetime literally if he took it then he wasn't allowed to do any other jobs ever. I guess he had no choice but to take it. He was to play "Stalin" at all Stalin's public appearances and photo opportunities. Stalin wasn't a pretty man. He got far because he knew about being good looking.

Now everyone knows about being good looking. I youtubed Toto's "Rains down in Africa" and figured that there's no way those guys could have a big hit like that today. They weren't good looking enough.

Music Speaks At Me

Do you know that sometimes when a popular song plays on the radio people think that the lyrics make a lot of sense and are really meaningful and really true to life. But when the song writer makes the song words up they just sit around smoking cigarettes and eating business lunches thinking about new sports cars and trying to think of a new 'do-wop' or a word that rhymes with baby or sexy or wild or some other word that is stupid. And do you think that when people hear songs they wish they could live like how it sounds like rock n' roll, wearing denim and leather and sunglasses and being dirty, smoking cigarettes and drinkin' hard and all that, with drugs and cheap hotels and not enough money to eat nice food. They don't even like food. They prefer cigarettes and cowboy boots. If that's the case then hip hop makes people wish they were really rich and had ladies and cars and furs and houses and respect and booty (rear end kind). In hip hop you don't have to smoke cigarettes but it helps to use cocaine and smoke weed so you can be mad lifted.

But mostly you try not to smoke crack
cause that's usually wack. Sometimes
music speaks to me but mostly I just like
to watch, I mean listen and sing along,
maybe dance but I'm pretty much white
so I can't dance really well. But that's OK
cause I don't have to do it for money or
anything.

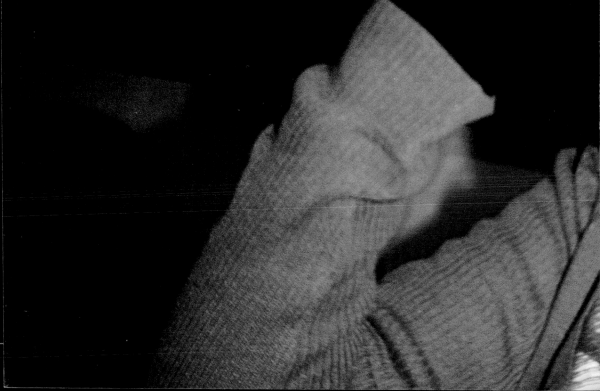

Chinese Restaurant

Chinese Waiter: So what were you up to tonight? Have you been at the tennis? (while pouring tea)

Customer: No we just went to see a film.

Chinese Waiter: Where did you go?

Customer: The Lumiere – you know, the art house cinema around the corner.

Chinese Waiter: Yeh, I went there once I saw Kill Bill. But actually that was the second time I went to see that movie. What did you see tonight?

Customer: A documentary about the Ramones – do you know the rock band?

Chinese Waiter: Yeah I know The Ramones but I don't really like rock and roll music. I like grunge music like Nirvana. I don't listen to anything else. I haven't listened to any new music in 10 years. I just really like grunge, I can really understand it in here (pounding his heart with his right hand). I have all their albums, I even have bootleg albums. You know when I listen to the music I can really understand Kurt, I know what he was thinking. I can feel his sadness and his honesty (his eyes start to get shiny like he might cry).

Customer: Yeh, Nirvana were a good band.

Chinese Waiter: Have you seen the Metallica movie?

Customer: No, but I know the one you mean – have you seen it?

Chinese Waiter: No I don't really like metal. I like Bon Jovi more and I like some of the Guns and Roses songs too... I have a lot of CD's but no new stuff. There's been no good new stuff in the last 10 years. Now I am listening more to jazz, 60's music and classic stuff like Suede. I like 90's British music. I like early Oasis and Blur & all that old stuff. I feel like I'm 40 which is sad because I'm only 28.

We are located in Mexico

We are located in Mexico, and we currently have close to 750,000 MT of Zinc Oxide ready to be shipped.

We are pretty sure they are stealing on demand, they are obviously hired guns of an organized gang who are very into fashion.

Our main products include:
Seafood: Black tiger, shrimp, fish, green crab, sardines canned, etc
Handicraft: Handbag, bamboo/seagrass/rattan/wood furniture, straw hat, basket, photo & picture frame, lacquer picture, hand-made pottery, candle, wooden box, wooden gift, so on.

Sell of Mexican sauce for snacks, seafood and famous Michelada drink.

Cream

The record-breaking balloon, almost as large as one and one half football fields, carried the Cosmic Ray Energetics And Mass (CREAM) experiment. CREAM is designed to explore the supernova acceleration limit of cosmic rays, the relativistic gas of protons, electrons and heavy nuclei arriving at Earth from outside the solar system.

"We are really proud of our crew in Antarctica," said Danny Ball.

Theft

I steal from strangers.

Pictures and Text by Dolly Moehrle

I take their moments.

When they think they're unobserved, and they don't hear the shutter click.

I'm always drawn to the same things: couples in quiet moments. Parents and children. People looking at other people. Children in the throes of deeply felt emotions, otherwise known as tantrums. Is this the female in me? Would a man be drawn to the titillating, to the powerful, rather than to the quiet and personal?

Or is it the human, the desire to connect to others, to take a bit of their lives and see my own in it? To see my own loneliness or anger or love or need or calm or curiosity ...

I never know what it is I've taken until later. It's a mystery until I hold it in my hands: a piece of a stranger's life, and they'll never know I have it.

Feeling is Believing
... And Developing

Pictures and Text by Elena Kulikova

Being a woman is a beautiful gift, and I love that with the feminine side I have received many emotions ... Women are feelers ... And it's a perfect gift, because I think it's better to feel with your heart, than to rationalize with settings ingrained in our heads ... And now it's not just women, people all over realize that feeling, following one's heart, is the right choice.

If you look at your own phases of development and stages of growth, and then observe your friends, you should see a collective development and the growth stage of our whole human existence. We're not just anomalies of each other, we're one collective being. And it's not just you who thinks this, and its not just me, I didn't even author it, it's our authoring.

Paris je t'aime

Pictures and Text by Gisela Davico

I close my eyes
and the hypnotic
cadenza of dancing
images of your streets
cafes and corners
is still lost in my mind,
in a sweet lethargy,
whispering, murmuring:
"Paris ... Paris ... Paris
Je t'aime, Je t'aime"

Wandering through
the narrow streets,
without company,
my loneliness I feel.
I still think about him,
call him in deep silence.
Paris, overwhelming city,
embraces me so sweet
and the pain dissolves,
erasing this tragedy.

Sunday is My Favourite Day of the Week

Pictures and Text by Stephanie Vermaas

Sunday is my favorite day of the week. Not because it falls on the weekend. Perhaps it's because it always seems like the sunniest day, and the sun never fails to put a smile on my face. I just know that when you live in Bali, every Sunday means a beach outing. It has grown into somewhat of a routine and I'm not so much into those, especially when routines revolve around work and meetings. But my Sunday routine does

not feel like a routine at all. Even Gisi, my dog, gets excited and runs circles around the car as soon as he sees us walking out of the gate. My beach bag is a dead give away of the fun to come, it is fully loaded with goodies to help me soak up as much of the sun as possible. My boyfriend is at my side, equipped with his board, ready to hit the waves. As soon as the car is unlocked, Gisi is the first one to jump in, and we are quick to

follow. He knows that it's Sunday, and it's a special day for him too, frolicking in the water, and chasing after a thrown ball are at the top of his hit list for the day. When we choose to rise to the occasion, which is just about always, we usually go old school ... Although Janis is old, she still has the power in her to gas up and down the hills of Bukit to reach our destination, Balangan, a beach tucked behind the cliffs of the

peninsula. It is our usual spot for sun worship. Leaving our house, we always pass the famous crazy old man from Canggu. This time he was just sitting and watching the traffic pass. He's been there for as long as I can remember. He definitely does not have the luxury to think of Sunday the way I do, because to him it's just another day of surviving without a home. It makes me a little sad every time we pass. I switch to my

favorite album, a Bob Marley staple that is perfect for cruising around with the windows down, as we drive pass strips of beautiful rice paddies. I see villagers working intensely in the field under the harsh glare of the sun. Sunday to them means work and striving to get rice on the table to feed their hungry family, even for the lady in pink, who hides her adversity underneath her straw hat. Sometimes I wish I could be in their shoes for a day, just to know how they feel. Halfway through Natty Dread, we reach the rocky path down to Balangan. A mini van is parked on top of the cliff with loud music blaring from its speakers surrounded by a crowd filled with young and old alike, dancing to the beat of the music. They are having a kick ass time. And how can they not? From the top, the beach is breathtaking, sunrays reflecting in the crystal blue water that ripples into perfect waves which break upon the reef. Yes it is a perfect day. Without hesitation my boyfriend left me for the surf and I find myself on my sun chair, already being hassled by the DVD guy who trawls the beach searching for customers, he claims his prices are the best. I politely refuse. Ironically this beach where I seek my peace and relaxation, is his market and I shouldn't blame him for wanting to earn

a buck or two. Life is hard here for the locals and sometimes we forget to see it and respect it. I always get philosophical on the beach and think about life. The thumping sound of the waves sends me into a deep trance as I submerge myself into a myriad of thoughts. As low tide approached, I decided to walk Gisi down to the water. The soft reef felt good massaging my feet. Gisi was running up and down, playing with tiny pools of water. That dog couldn't be much happier. I must admit, me too! I've never felt so lucky to be here as I do right now. The sun slowly disappeared from the horizon and the sky turned into an array of colours as the week concludes to an end. I enjoyed the dazzling view. I felt so carefree in that moment. And it makes me forget about everything else. Life is beautiful.

Coming and Going

Pictures and Text by Emma Kidd

Why is it that the women are the ones that generally follow?

Four years ago I agreed to move to the North of France from Australia. Many reasons. I had gone back and forth from France over the five years preceding this move, but never longer than a tourist visa would allow.

I found myself in a "ghost town" (as Lille is in Summer), wondering what the hell I had agreed to. No sea nearby, no friends, an adopted family that didn't really know me and a big language barrier.

I have since met many women virtually and in person who have told me a similar story. It can be strange and alienating. I felt like I lost my personality for those first three years. I have now claimed it back as I have learnt the language (not perfect, but passable) and met people who are my friends and not my man's.

I am about to move back to Australia,
but having been here for this time,
France has grown inside me. I understand the pride in their culture that is
mistaken, quite frequently, for arrogance.
I enjoy their quirks and expressiveness.
I will miss it, but it's not going anywhere.
It will be here when I next come back.
I need to live my life. Anyway, I have my
piece of France with me that is following
me back to Australia.

This Old House

Pictures and Text by Jillian Pichocki

When we met 7 years ago there were some necessary milestones leading up to when we would get married. Among them was finishing grad school (which I did last year) ... the another being when he bought this house. It is going on close to eight years now of not knowing what are we going to do. The house is old and in dire need of repair. But that requires money that we do not have. Piece by piece we are constructing these changes while along the way trying to make definitive plans as to our future together. All the objects lying around the house remind me that it is his house, while I constantly try to find my place in it. We bought an old organ from a thrift store. More and more I am trying to become a part of that house, even I do not physically live in it (yet?). Everything in it is a reminder as to how complicated our relationship is. Often, I find myself wondering what could be said of the previous owners if the walls could talk, but then I grow more curious as to what would be said about us.

So Young, Broken Doll

Pictures and Text by Zita Vehil

So old, so ugly, the lost beautiful dreamer. Not yet so beautiful, just a distortion of the illusions of her youth. Like pieces of a giant collage, that never make the perfect wall, but actually show a sad and pathetic obsession. The cutest lady is vanishing, but she'll never know. What does the mirror says? Who is the prettiest of them all?

We all are pieces; pieces that are inside our body and outside too. A piece of a naughty smile that sounded loud and happy in the past, now it is a memory, like when we put on those old and broken pantyhose, or something that reminds us of our childhood. Many pieces everywhere, that sometimes are a part of broken dreams, hearts or hopes.

There's a certain madness in our way to see the world. We have to *be something better* every day. Not someone special, but a pretty girl, a good housewife, a happy and quiet old woman ... But the truth is that we want to walk on the wild side, being freaks, or odd, or something worse, Mae West. I want to be old-fashioned, ugly and without a boyfriend; I want to be alone. Watching the people while they walk down the street. I would be reading a book, or writing it.

My mama is right now a result of a little and naughty young girl, a cute and pretty woman, a fabulous cooker and housewife, a virginal lover and a busy mother: she is under the sun, catching the glitter of the summer, telling me that I'm pretty, that I have a wonderful body, and that I could have all the handsome boys I want, but who cares, mom? I don't want to be another face broken on a dusty wall!

A Never-ending Film Roll

Pictures and Text by Ayu Peeters

Truthfully I bought the Diana F+ completely based on how it looks, I couldn't take my eyes off of her. It was love at first sight. As I got home I was eager to play with her and take her with me on the adventures I was sure we would share.
After a while it felt like a daily addiction taking photos and I couldn't get rid of it.

When I look at my photos now, I can feel the connection between Diana, the subject and me.
I see that I have captured a moment from running away, an instant in time that intrigued me, and now I am able to look back at it and reminisce on that particular feeling I was going through at that time. Every photo is a memory telling a sort of reality fairytale, except this fairytale is a never ending story.

Roll after roll I can feel the excitement build up in me curious about what the Diana is going to show me. I never have expectations on how the photographs should look like, but one thing I know for sure is she is always full of surprises.

The perfect moment might not always be the perfect picture but it's that imperfection that gives charisma, beauty and character, all at the same time. Something so simple with so many possibilities of experimentation will keep me busy exploring all of the excitement around me.

Not only is she the best sidekick I can carry around me but she is always ready to Rock n' Roll with me wherever and whenever. I cannot be anymore satisfied with my dazzling plastic lens, just like Affandi would say, "I do the art, not because I like to be rich, not because I like to be famous, but because I have to. The calling of the soul".

A Letter for Whoever

Pictures and Text by Andrew Kua

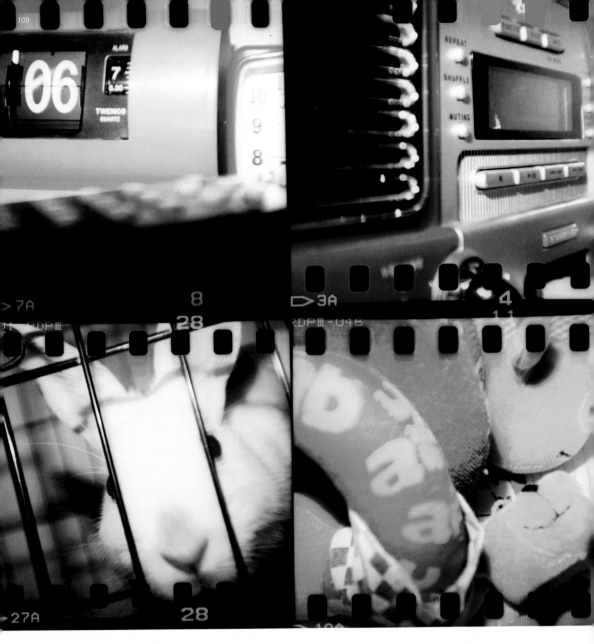

Dear husband,

There are some things that I've always wanted to tell you but you are always complaining that I nag too much. Oh well, since you often say that a picture paints a thousand words, I'll use these photos to say what I wanna say.

(Hey, if you can stand a thousand words from each photo, why are you complaining that I'm nagging when I only repeat 10 words a couple of times?!)

First ... for God's sake, don't wake me up when you can't sleep! I ain't the one who made you drink a bucket of double espresso before bed time!

Next, please note that not everyone loves Metallica as much as you do. The whole family (excluding you of course!) needs some peace at home and you better stop blasting your music that loud. The family staying 10 floors below could easily record what you were playing and burn them into a CD instead of downloading illegally on the internet.

The pet rabbit needs food! Don't think that she'll be able to survive on beer and nachos like you do, so please ... feed the poor bugger when I'm not at home!

Please stop buying toys for our boy, as we do not have enough room to store them. Toys'R'Us doesn't need to depend on you alone to generate revenue. Save some money for rabbit food okay?

Oh, and that darn robot toy you bought last week ... it makes really scary sound and has horrible blinking red and blue eyes. Not sure if you'll believe this, just the other night I had a dream of it chasing me around the block. Damn! Trash it, will ya?

Stop complaining about the food I prepare. You are a lump of fat walking around and you should be eating more vegetables. Don't ask me why ain't we serving steak for dinner tonight! I don't mind the insurance payout but I don't think I have the strength to drag your dead body to the hospital.

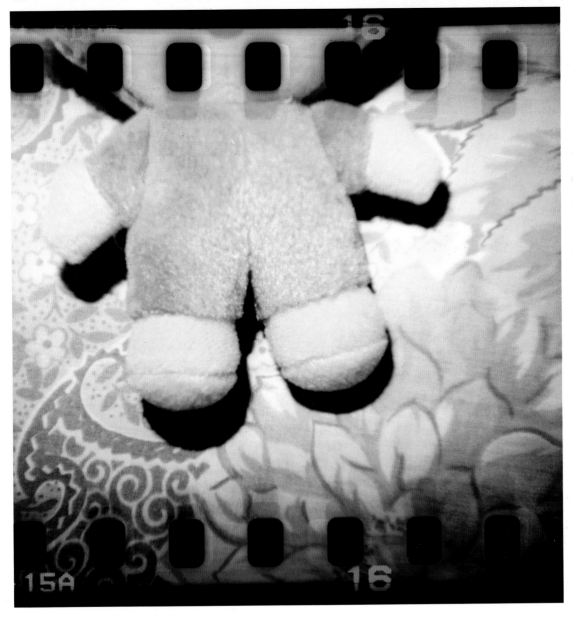

I told you not to waste money on buying flowers for my birthday, but that doesn't mean you can send me fake plastic flowers. Geddit???

Oh, by the way ... the credit card company called and said you've exceeded your credit limit. I think you should stop buying that many plastic cameras or else we'll have to mortgage our house to pay for your cameras!

Hope you have a great day at work, you BIG FAT MONKEY!

Love,

The wife

We Met on a Beach

Pictures and Text by Alex Lyons

We met on a beach in the Mediterranean, I miss you, even as I lie here taking it all in. Your foot prints next to mine in the sand, the way the sand stuck to your messy hair. At first you talked a lot of rubbish to me, how you liked my style and the way I combed my hair and stuff, but I was cool, but I just ran with it, went with the flow, just like the river we sat next to.

You liked to embarrass me on every public outing we took together, you jumped in fountains, you urinated in fountains, you ran around naked, you got spaghetti all over your top, but, through all this, you didn't care, so you know what, I didn't care either.

You called yourself an artist, sorry, a street artist. You drummed that into my head, love for the streets and all that jazz. You had a strange obsession with sun glasses, you wore them with pride, but you lost or broke a pair on most outings. You took me on an adventure to Napoli to go to some jazz clubs, you took me on the back of a Vespa, you wore all yellow for precaution.

You took me to a fancy pizzeria you got salami on your top. You left your mark on the walls of Napoli, then you ran away and left me there.

Disharmonic Mind

Pictures and Text by Satomi Sugiyama

Adventurous, I want to be.

Bad-tempered, I can't help but to be.

Coincidences, I truly adore.

Disappointed, in myself.

Egomaniacs, stay away.

Fortune-tellers, what's my fate?

Global warming – end of the world.

Hypocrites, lying again.

Imprisoned, in my dream.

Judgmental – how I am.

Kind-hearted ... well, sometimes.

Longing for the good-old-days.

Materialistic – what I have become?

Nerve-wracking, the world of today.

Optimistic – If I could be.

Photographing, the beauty of life.

Questioning, my own self.

Right or wrong – who am I to judge?

Step by step, I find my way.

Treasuring all the people I love.

Understanding, who I am.

Visualize my own future.

With you, I can grow old.

X-mas, so many more to come.

Year by year, our love will grow.

Zodiac sign can't tell who I am.

A to Z, I am what I am.

Shirley Bell

Pictures and Text by Lauren Maxfield

I lost you at 10:30.

When I came back, through your front door, I found that the clock had stopped too. Your house was so silent.

You were the grandfather's guardian, everyday, making sure it was wound; you would pull out the tiny key, nestle it into the clock's gold face, and spin it as the weights ascended, all the way up, almost out of sight.

You were a keeper, a matriarch of time.

Sometimes I would lay with you, and we would talk and listen to the clock on its way, marching further and further into the night, and we would fall asleep in its path.

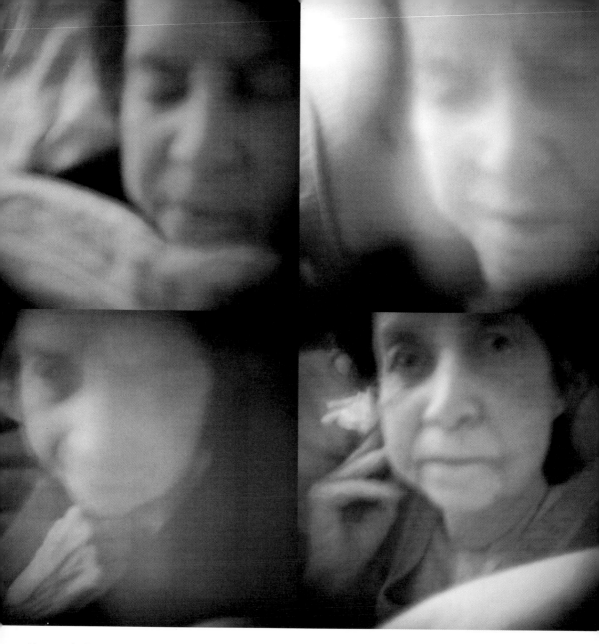

I became the keeper of your last moments, my little plastic box receiving
your light, drawing you out of your bed
and your body, making sure you were
captured.

The clock is in my house now. I can hear
you in it. A viscous beating in my ears,
behind my eyes, every time it calls. My
grandmother clock.

How I Became a Photographer
or Teaching Birds to Draw

Pictures and Text by Annette Fournet

One day I woke up and everything was different. Like Alice in Wonderland the world presented itself as an unknown and magical realm. Rather than falling down a rabbit hole it seems I had sprouted like a seed in the garden. From somewhere deep inside a desire had germinated to change my life and had pushed up from my subconscious to cognizance. New adventures and an untold number of things to accomplish waited for me on the horizon of my life. I quit my job in the dark and dank Ink Factory. Considering the earthy nature of my epiphany I first thought I might become a horticulturist. I dwelled in the woods, hunted mushrooms, communed with the forest folk and tended my small garden. Tranquility filled my days. Alas, it was not enough to keep me fulfilled and perhaps working in the dirt was not my true passion. I pondered my next move and decided at long last that I had found my calling, to teach birds to draw. This was somewhat more difficult than one might think and, in point of fact, the birds seemed very disinclined to learn the basic principals of design. Sadly, I said au revoir to my avian atelier. I consulted the want ads of the Herald Tribune. The next opportunity that presented itself to me was to join the Chinese Opera. My ascent was swift.

The critics' accolades were gratifying. Being a star in Beijing was delightful and exciting, but really just not pour moi! I knew my destiny was out there somewhere in this wild new world but what was it? I packed up and began to travel the world accompanied by my trusty Diana+ Cameras. First I went to Greece and was overwhelmed by colossal ruins, then on to China to see old friends and to document their lives. Visiting Japan was an inspiring journey and gave me insight into the aesthetic of wabi-sabi. From Praha to Paris I photographed it all and loved every minute of it. Finally I understood my true vocation was photography! I recognized that my destiny had been discovered, my fortune made and my life was on track. This is how I became a photographer.

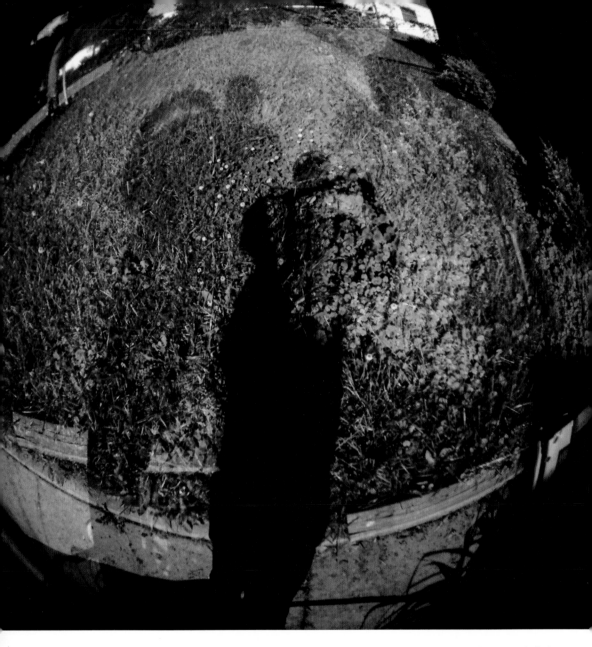

Dazed and Disengaged

Pictures and Text by Adrienne Jones

Hello, my name is Adrienne and I feel like a shadow. I have been unemployed since January 2008. I'll explain …

I hated my job of (nearly) 10 years. When offered a chance to leave – I did. Without another gig waiting for me.

So, I did what I'd meant to for years past, and left the big buildings of downtown behind.

I'm often scared, angry, confused, sad.

The nightmares started in March. Zombies, vampires, visions of apocalypse fill my already frightened head.

My husband sleeps soundly and offers hope.

While the bright colors have disappeared for me.

Even when I'm happy, I can feel things crumbling.

I'm trying. Every social networking site and job search bank knows my name and what I've done before.

And yet, since January ... only two interviews and one (barely) part time freelance job – taking pictures and writing.

A week long honeymoon at the beach eased my mind briefly.

Forgetting would be great. Flying away or taking public shots at idiots who refuse to hire me? Even better.

Now and since that trip the world is cold and hard again.

Do I take another years-long crap job?
Or do I continue to hold out for meaningful work? Oprah cannot be the only
one who gets to live her dreams.

Unemployment ends mid-December.
Time will soon tell.

(1)

The Weekend

Pictures and Text by Fabienne Elisabeth

(2)

(3)

(4)

(5)

Getting up early on weekends can also make you happy.

After running all week, working crazy, trying to have a social life, groaning about all this time lost in the subway ... (1)

... Here comes the week-end, my time at last, YES!

But NO, so many things are waiting for me ...

Like many other women, I have to get up early on Saturday to go to the market (2) while my man still sleeps, lucky one! Which means not enough sleep for me, being nice with people you don't know ...

But, in the end, I start to enjoy this new routine, seeing this delicious food all around, even the I-shouldn't-eat-this Italian cheese that is calling for me ... (3)

And even the salesman's smile, he knows me now and gently teases me about my puffy eyes ... (at this moment I am so glad my man's not there). (4)

(6)

Well, I guess I can finally find some pleasure in what I thought of first as a chore ...

Then I think I can rest ... spending a nice Sunday doing nothing ...

But NO! I have to go celebrate my father's birthday a good hour driving from my home, ... So I get up early, again, on Sunday, how cruel is that? Still my man lays in bed saying he's feeling sick, hmmm I feel a lie behind this but what can I say?

When I arrive, I find some champagne waiting to be shared by the people I love (5), I spend some time talking with my 95 year old grandpa, the whole time I am so grateful, I do realize how lucky I am that he still lives (6), and as I'm in the countryside I can even try to take some nice sunny pictures ... (7)

Then I'm off home, at last, some time for myself?

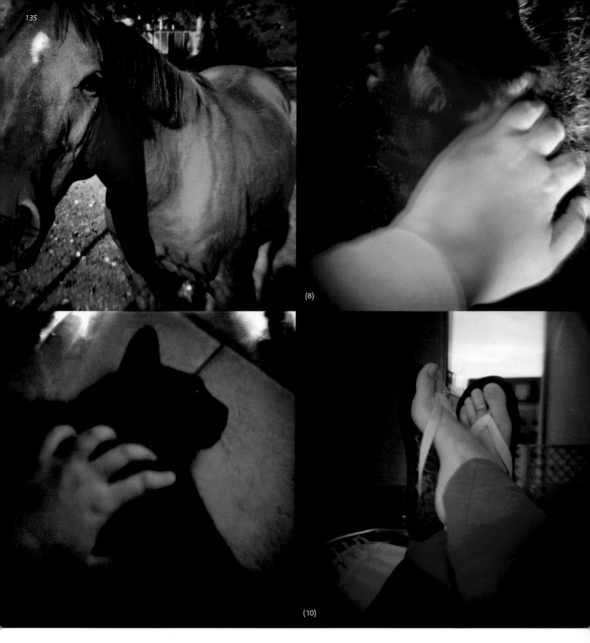

(8)

(10)

NO! My cats are waiting for me, asking, demanding for my presence (8, 9), which reminds me that I have to clean the litter, run to the nearest grocery open on Sunday because I forgot to buy their food ... And of course my man, still claiming illness, has done nothing ...

Then, at last, Sunday evening arrives, I finally find some time to sit on my deckchair, relaxing, and enjoying doing nothing ... what I've waited for the whole week-end ... (10)

YES I had not too much time for myself, but if I step back and look at it, I was able to experience such simple, precious, unexpected moments of happiness.

I had no time to lie in bed, (are we women cursed and doomed to never enjoy that guilty pleasure?) but I had a wonderful weekend, as always.

Stories from the Lens, Stories from the Life

Pictures and Text by Lucía deMosteyrín

My world is a barrel of chaos, full of all sort of experiences and such good feelings and good people ... My world cannot be represented in a film, nor in a book or even a drawing, but sometimes, only sometimes, it can be glimpsed within a Lomopic taken by myself. My life.

Sometimes destructive, sometimes pro-gressing. But always my vehicle in which to live the moments. To breath the souls. To know the whole earth.

These pics show my vision of my city and the people and things that live in it. You may find stress and hard times, but there are fairy tales as well. Hidden behind a corner of whores or walking around a neighbourhood of posh fami-lies, you can find it all.

My life and my mind can only fit inside a Lomo camera. Over the film drawn by it.

I introduce you to my real live. Come in and please take a seat.

Delicious Diana!

Pictures and Text by Stefanie Sourial

My Name is Stefanie Sourial.
Yes, you pronounce it "surreal".
I am Egyptian and grew up in a very
small town in Austria, called Wachau.

When I turned 18, I decided to move to
Paris, to experience and find something
new. From everything I expected it to
be, I would have never imagined what I
really found there.

I encountered new tastes and smells and realized a huge fascination and obsession with these phenomena. I could not get enough of the food and their vibrant flavours.

Having always been quite a social and chatty person, I started to go on a culinary journey for almost a year all by myself ... and then, I got carried away.

The reason for this new found passion is not that I did not enjoy the food back home, but you see, for me food at home was always less interesting because I already knew it, I already knew the tastes and smells, and was especially familiar with the consistency.

I can remember every single time I have had an encounter with a new kind of consistency; like as a child and biting for the first time into a pure and thick mass of marzipan, or the heart of an artichoke, or the thick dough of a pretzel. Pretzel dough always reminded me of the kind of bread that Vicky the Viking (or in French: Vic le Viking) would eat.

However, coming to Paris, I fell into a glut of infinitesimal gastronomical delights, new tastes and flavours. I went from store to store, testing everything. I found my first street market, and devoured the entirescene, watching crazy people selling their crazy clothes, crazy costumes, old vinyl and vintage furniture.

I would always pass by and follow the smell of fresh bread and one day, there it was: a stand, run by a freelance pastry cook, who, on that day, sold her home-made macarons.

Macaroons.
I remember spending almost an hour in front of that stand, tasting each of her flavours.

My noises of pleasure and absolute devotedness made other pedestrians stop and rediscover what they already knew so well. Watching me made them think that perhaps this culinary genius had created something new.

Of course that was not the case at all, I just discovered something that had completly overwhelmed me.

Madame Flora and her macaroons.
She said:
"I know, Cherie, I know, eating this is like having the view of a beautiful river valley, but above all, it is all dyed in wonderful pink."

Of course I bought a whole box to take with me and ...
Just a moment – sticking to that phenomenon of the box:

Confectioners in Austria put cakes into a paper bag, which is not the best solution, especially, when you have a long way to go before getting home. Opening the bag after that journey always turned out to be a big disappointment, as the cream would not be inside the pies anymore, but all over the paper.

The box would not let such a thing happen.

The box has two pros:
First of all:
It protects its insides, the way it should be protected. The way my ribs protect my lungs, my stomach and my heart.
Second of all:
It is beautiful and makes you want to see what there is hidden and buried inside of it.

It peaks your desire to open it, like Pandora had to open her box, or ... and I know I am going very far now, but to hell with it, why not:
"Pulp Fiction's" famous suitcase:
I truly believe that Quentin Tarantino MUST have thought about a beautiful cardboard box full of the most delicious pastries when he had the idea of that mysterious briefcase and the way it glowed, whenever anybody opened it.

At least, I always have that expression on my face, when I open a box of macaroons.

I still do!

Madame Flora does not exist anymore, but you should, whenever you have the chance, go to "Marché sur la Place Monge", where you will find the most outstanding macaroons in one of those bakeries, where Rue Monge crosses Rue Lacepede.

Bon appetit!

Coincidence

Pictures and Text by Margherita Cecchini

These are the days of miracle and wonder.
Paul Simon

I recognize something that I had never seen until that moment, that is beyond all my intentions:

I look back at all these photos I have accumulated ... moments of awakening, split seconds, a slow motion rough cut from a film, which I have been living by proxy, more from outside than inside ...

Is it dreams that my photographs are about? Or even better, are they hallucinations?

It was summer, it was Sunday, I passed by over there, I shoot. Coincidence.

Sarah Moon

colette
Contributors

Claw Money (US)

Queens-born Claw Money first made a name for herself on the street-art scene. She is now a fashion editor of Swindle magazine and a designer of her own clothing and accessories line. Most recently Claw has been on a world tour promoting sneaker collaborations with the sport's giant Nike. This first artist release for women by a woman sets a new precedent for female street wear collaborations in an extremely male dominated market.
www.clawmoney.com

Daphné Bürki (FR)

Journalist. Specialist in new trends and styles. Daphne currently hosts "L'édition spéciale" on French TV channel Canal+ every day at 12:25pm. Previously she worked as a stylist for John Galliano/ Dior for two years. Daphné began her career as an art student working as an animator for birthday parties.
Profile: active, spontaneous, positive
Slogan: Have Fun

Picture by Robert Mc Kim

Jenny Mannerheim (FR)

Based in Paris since 2002, Stockholm-born Jenny has worked as an art director for various magazines including Numéro, Standard, Muteen, Vogue Hommes International and Beaux Arts magazine. In 2004 Jenny launched Nuke magazine and opened her own gallery in Paris, Galerie Nuke. Nuke 'Generation Polluée' is an art magazine for artists, designers and writers. It's not a journalistic magazine and does not targeting critics, the market, etc. Jenny develops Nuke magazine and Gallery Nuke in conjunction with her profession as an art director.
Since 2006 Jenny has also been the Art Director of the huge contemporary art book series "Made by ..." published by Enrico Navarra and directed by Fabrice Bousteau.
www.nuke.fr
www.galerienuke.fr

Linlee Allen (US)

Australian-born writer/photojournalist Linlee Allen is currently residing in Los Angeles. In addition to photograph-ing colorful characters on her blog at linleeloves.blogspot.com she also con-tributes to www.style.com, V magazine and countless other publications as a west coast correspondent.

Shauna T (AU)

Based in Melbourne, Australia, Shauna T designs art, makes art and makes a whole lotta other cool things too. Shauna T is one half of cult brand PAM, which creates clothing, graphics and small art books. She is also a member of the international art band, The Changes, with short stories published in Doing Bird magazine. Shauna T and husband, Misha, own a store called "Someday" in Melbourne.
www.perksandmini.com
www.someday-store.com

Fafi (FR)

Fafi is notorious for painting and hustling, her sexy, funny, and sometimes aggressive girl characters; by exploring feminity through stereotypes, and using it to her advantage, she drew enormous attention and thus started to travel the world with thousands of Fafinettes in her brushes and paint cans. Her multi-faceted work was all documented in her books GIRLS ROCK (2003) and LOVE AND FAFINESS (2006), both being also succesful prints in museum libraries and selected shops. Fafi started her career on the walls of Toulouse but is now a proud Paris dweller. www.fafi.net

Feride Uslu (DE)

Since the early 90s Feride has painted faces, shortly after 2000 she started up her own airline (Originally based out of New York, now Berlin), and since speaking with Lomography, she's going to be a photographer!
Feride Uslu – makeup artist/entrepreneuse www.usluairlines.com

Helena Ichbiah/Ich&Kar (FR)

Ich&Kar is an impertinently bold duet of graphic designers who create highly specialized and surprising visual effects on a variety of subjects. Ich&Kar's extensive and comprehensive experience covers a vast range of subjects from luxury to mass-market goods. Ich&Kar's global approach goes far and beyond a given subject through an innovative touch that encompasses meaning, sensuality and talent – a unique Midas' touch that turns the ordinary into the extraordinary. Ich&Kar's duo is formed by a man and a woman fully devoted to deepening the impact of messages through evocative and elusive imagery. Their priority is to imbed their messages in reality and develop the representation of the messages in a clear, straight-forward language that rises above that of fashion, gimmicks and superfluous-ness. Ich&Kar's goal is to convey meaning through humor and light-heartedness. www.ichetkar.com

Sophie Toporkoff (FR)

Sophie Toporkoff creates magazines (Rendez-Vous, Agenda), collaborates with great brands (including Maison Martin Margiela as their new Communication Art Director, colette, Kiehl's), artists (for Palais de Tokyo, Galerie Kamel Mennour) and musicians. Sophie also draws a lot. Always in search of a new idea or impulse, her eclectic body of work has continued to gain exposure over the last few years with solo exhibitions and installations at Allodi-R (Toyko), colette (Paris) and galerie La Bank (Paris).

Tommy (GB)

Hello. My name is Tommy. I live in London and I like beautiful things. www.thisisnaive.com

Lomography.com Contributors

Adrienne Jones (US)
www.lomohomes.com/monymann

I enjoy being the odd woman out; walking down the street photographing any and everything. I've recently gotten into collecting old cameras and my current count stands at 12, all in various states of usability. I shoot with my Diana+, Lomo Orbit 360F, two Polaroids and my Canon S3 IS. I live with my husband, Chaz, and our cat Tux, both of whom I love dearly (even though he often bites me – the cat that is). Special thanks goes to my godmother, Denise, for giving me my first camera (a Kodak Disk camera which I still have) for my 9th birthday!

Alex Lyons (GB)
www.lomohomes.com/alexroarsatlyons

Yo! I'm Alex from London I'm 18 years old and I like taking photos and drinking lots of milk. I have my own website www.alex-lyons.co.uk with lots more Lomography I have taken on my travels. I like to take a bag of film and a bunch of cameras and go on adventures with my friends!

Dolly Moehrle (US)
www.lomohomes.com/dmoehrle

While not swimming through the endless dreck produced by the aspiring screenwriters of Los Angeles, Dolly Moehrle nurses her hobby addiction. Her time is occupied variously by knitting, guitar, paper making, sewing, collecting vintage issues of "Superman's Girlfriend Lois Lane" comics, and futzing around with analogue cameras while everyone else has forgotten what film looks like. Primarily, though, she writes short stories about lovelorn girls and space aliens, novels about detectives and screenplays in which things blow up.

Elena Kulikova (US)
www.lomohomes.com/elena506

I am a young 23 year old woman, discovering herself in a pool of beauty as I find myself eternally at school. I am forever enrolled into lessons of the senses, a rise toward knowledge of self and universe and a better humanity, and this physical world in which we play in, a sandbox for the big kids, it's so fun. Thank you, everyone.

Emma Kidd (AU)
www.lomohomes.com/grifter

I am an Australian photographer/artist/illustrator who has always had a passion for film. I have just returned to Australia after four years in France. I wish I had a teleporter.

Andrew Kua (SG)
www.lomohomes.com/ndroo

Lomography and experimental photography lover from Singapore who probably spends more time (and money) on cameras and film than food, and was trapped in the digital craze until enlightenment came in the form of Lomography and film.

Annette Fournet (US)
www.lomohomes.com/radosti

Since 1989 I have been shooting exclusively with Diana Cameras. I am the proud owner of 72 Diana, Diana clone and Diana+ cameras. My photographs have been exhibited in France, Greece, Great Britain, Denmark, Czech Republic, Slovakia, Romania, Hungary, Poland and the United States.

Ayu Peeters (BE)
www.lomohomes.com/ommanipadmehum

I'm a mixture of expression and color the only thing that makes us different is: I am not made out of plastic!

Fabienne Elisabeth (FR)
www.lomohomes.com/fabyen

My name is Fabienne ELISABETH, I am a 36 years old French web designer working for a B2B communication company in Paris. Most of my free time (along with my boyfriend and cats!) is dedicated to analog photography, mostly Lomography which allows me to experiment with new stuff and have a lot of fun! My favorite cameras are Diana, Holga, and recently the LC-A ... Anything but digital, isn't that paradoxical regarding my completely digital job? ...
Feel free to visit my blog:
www.fabelis.over-blog.com

Gisela Davico (AR)
www.lomohomes.com/giseladavico

Gisela Davico, photographer, social researcher, chronic traveler, loves to unveil the beauty of the world through a lens.

Jillian Pichocki (US)
www.lomohomes.com/jillog

I am an avid analog enthusiast. I love all forms of photography ranging from plastic cameras to historical processes such as the daguerreotype. Working on the images for this project was different and exciting because it made me pick up DIANA and start to look at my own life as opposed to being so focused on others.

Lauren Maxfield (US)
www.lomohomes.com/thebrightness

lauren maxfield.aka.thebrightness.
photographer.vegan.sister.daughter.
sentient being.
Loves her family. Loves her dog and her
rats. Loves lightning, old ladies, banana
bread and plastic art.

Lucía deMosteyrín (ES)
www.lomohomes.com/mujer12balas

I am a Spanish Lomographer named
Lucía deMosteyrín. Photography is
my soul-consuming obsession, and
Lomography's a very important part of
it. I met this crazy world two years ago,
and I have become totally addicted to
this way of life since then. Pictures are
the only way of truly expressing myself:
my inner world, my deepest secrets, my
hidden madness … The Dianalogues of
my own life.

Margherita Cecchini (IT)
www.lomohomes.com/marghelomo

I am 32 years old and was born in Imola
(Bologna). After working in Manhattan as
a black and white printer, I returned to
Italy to work as a press photographer for
a local newspaper and as freelance photographer for various art projects and
exhibitions for magazines & commercial
projects. I am now with Cineteca/Bolo-
gna, Toscana Photographic Workshop/
Bologna (www.tpw.it), and have also
have had photos published with the Ki-
tao/Marka Agency, Milan (www.marka.it)
"D di Repubblica" magazine for women.
Also works for the magazine Premium/
Forlì (www.menabo.com). Education:
Photography Diploma from the Istituto
Europeo del Design, Milano, a.a. 1998/99.

Zita Vehil (ES)
www.lomohomes.com/blueliv

I'm from Barcelona, Spain. I studied
graphic design and now it is my job. I
love Lomography, and I can say without
no doubt that Lomography is an integral
part of my life, you know, "I lomo,
therefore I am". If you take a look at my
lomos you'll see through my eyes: the
sea in old black and white, the fauvist
skies, the blurred and distorted buildings,
the dreamy landscapes with light leaks,
and the pieces of lost people. I hope
that all these things will be reflected in
the pictures, and much more, try to find
your own face in them!

Satomi Sugiyama (JP)
www.lomohomes.com/satomi

Stefanie Sourial (AUT)
www.lomohomes.com/stretzen4snog

Stephanie Vermaas (ID)
www.lomohomes.com/vstephanie

My name is Satomi Sugiyama, and I am a Lomo-bot, made in Japan. My mission began after I was shipped to the states in the year 2000, and I have been on a Lomographic rampage ever since.
Status: Analogue photography is on the verge of extinction due to the digital virus that has spread rapidly among humans.
Current Mission: Save the world from the digital infection.

Born in 1981, I still have my baby teeth. I am that kind of a person who gets up at 5:30 a.m. in the morning to bake bread. February I swim in the North Sea, March it is the Atlantic Ocean, and last November I swam in the Danube.
I hate sports and I am the "the second" co-founder of the jelly-dance.
My name is Gene and I am a Kelly.
My name is Heathcliff and I am a Huxtable.
My name is Ruth and that's the truth.

I wake up everyday with the aroma of incense and an offering on my doorstep. Occasionally I sit in traffic, because of ceremony. I get chased by street dogs late at night. I'm just a girl living in a third world paradise that they call the island of the gods.

The Lomographic Society // How Everything Started

What the Hell is Lomography

In the early 1990s, a handful of Viennese students took a trip to Prague and happened upon a small enigmatic Russian camera called the Lomo Kompakt Automat. Immediately, they started a new style of artistic experimental photography using their unorthodox snapshot cavortings. Their approach: Take as many photographs (Lomographs) as possible in the most impossible of situations possible and from the most unusual positions possible and having them developed as cheaply as possible. The result was a flood of authentic, colorful, crazy, off-the-wall, and unfamiliar snapshots, which could be combined and mounted on panels to form a sea of thousands of Lomographs. Lomographic events, exhibitions, and interactive projects were soon rolled out across the world, and Lomographic "Embassies" were founded in over 75 countries. To date, major shows have been held in Moscow, New York, Vienna, Berlin, St. Petersburg, Paris, Shanghai, Guangzhou, Bangkok, Kuala Lumpur, Sidney, Melbourne, Sao Paolo, Rio de Janeiro, Mexico City, Guadalajara, Medelin, Toronto, Oslo, Stockholm, Malmö, Helsinki, Cape Town, Johannesburg, Seoul, Havana, Zurich, Cologne, Madrid, Cairo, Frankfurt, Dubai, Oslo, Tokyo, Hong Kong, Singapore, Buenos Aires, London, Barcelona, Beijing, and many other cities. In fact, you might want to cast a quick glance at www.lomography.com/events to see what's going down at this very moment.

Lomography
People, Lifestyle, and Tools

What started out as a spontaneous artistic approach to photography in the Vienna underground scene developed into an international socio-cultural movement, one that uses photography as a creative approach for capturing the world – and for communicating with others. Today, we are a globally active organization dedicated to experimental and creative snapshot photography. Boasting more than 500,000 active members across the world, the idea of Lomography encompasses an interactive, democratic, social, cultural, vivid, blurred, and crazy way of life.

This development is supported and furthered by the creation of special tools that were either discovered or specifically designed and manufactured. We're mostly talking affordable snapshot cameras like the Lomo LC-A+, the Diana+ & Diana F+, the four-lensed Supersampler & Actionsampler, the Colorsplash and Fisheye cameras, and the Holga and Horizon cameras. But there's also a whole assortment of accessories, including flashes, tripods, films, bags, notebooks, albums, frames, in-house published books; and fashion items to discover as well. Check out the whole assortment on www.lomography.com.

Lomography & Visual Culture

The social and visual credo of Lomography has influenced lots of different people – from cultural gurus and creative types to business people, educators, and other professionals. Among these strident supporters and Lomographic camera shooters are quite a few celebrities and well-known creative types, such as Moby, David Byrne, LCD Soundsystem, Vladimir Putin, Master Yuen, Underworld, Giovanni Ribisi, Nobuyoshi Araki, Eason Chan (The King of Canton Pop), Franz Ferdinand, Dalek, Eve, Anton Corbijn, Daft Punk, Danny Clinch, Nikki Sixx, Staple Design, Rosie O'Donnell, Kareem Black, The Cold War Kids, Jeanne Tripplehorn, Yonehara Yasumasa, Radiohead, Grizzly Bear, John Vanderslice, Mark Romanek, Jason Lee, Shepard Fairey, Kirsten Dunst, The White Stripes, Kozyndan, Eva Mendes, Bady Minck, the Leningrad Cowboys, and Meatloaf. So you're in good company!

The Lomographic credo – "be fast, be open-minded, be communicative" – has spread into an approach that is shared throughout the Lomographic network. This special premise is based on the playful combination of lo-tech and hi-creativity, and the amalgamation of a cultural institution with a commercial photographic and design company. This grants our Lomographic Society an exquisite role in this age of borderless global telecommunications wherever images and visual language are involved.

The Lomography World Archive & Lomography.com

Where is all of this going? We are busy-beavering away with hundreds of thousands of Lomographers on the perpetually ongoing Lomographic Sisiphus project: The Lomography World Archive. This archive seeks to document the incredible world around us in a never-ending stream of snapshots, and we hope to make it the biggest and most dazzling snapshot collection on Earth, a collection of millions of the wackiest, most exciting, and most impressive sights and moments of our time! Where are these archives? Inside the shoe boxes of Lomographers, stacked on chairs or tables, in cupboards, drawers, albums, on the ceilings and walls, cataloged on computer hard drives, in the vast collections of the Lomographic Embassies and at the Lomographic Society International Central Archive in Vienna ... and in the highest & most selective quality at the online LomoWorldArchive at www.lomography.com/archive. It's an archive that's growing by the minute!

Join us (the Lomographers), and discover all the events, competitions, activities, products, and inspirational bits and pieces that we offer. We can't wait to meet you!

Our international website:
www.lomography.com

The extremely receptive and gregarious e-mail address for all of your questions:
contact@lomography.com

Lomographic Society Offices Worldwide

Hey, if you're ever in the neighborhood, then feel free to pop by one of our warm-hearted Lomographic offices. Bring your personal Lomographic portfolio, some baked goods or an extremely cute puppy and you're guaranteed to catch us in a fantastic mood.

Europe
Lomographic Society International
Hollergasse 41,
A-1150 Vienna
tel: +43.1.899 44 0
fax: +43.1.899 44 22
contact@lomography.com

USA
Lomographic Society USA
41W 8th Street
10011 New York, NY
tel: +1.212.529 43 53
fax: +1.212.529 43 60
info-usa@lomography.com

Korea
Lomographic Society Korea
705 Greenville 1601-2,
1F Seogyo-Dong Mapo-Gu,
121-838 Seoul, South Korea
tel: +82.2.522 02 55
fax: +82.2.523 02 55
www.lomography.co.kr

Japan
Lomographic Society Japan
4-24-8 Minamiaoyama, 3F
Minato-Ku, Tokyo, 107-0062
tel: +81.3.6418 78 67
fax: +81.3.6418 78 93
www.lomography.jp

Hong Kong
Lomography Asia Pacific Ltd.
G/F, No. 2, Po Yan Street, Sheung Wan,
Hong Kong
tel: +852.2525 54 17
fax: +852.2525 54 67
info@lomographyasia.com

1. Take your camera **everywhere** you go

2. Use it **any time** – day and night

3. Lomography is not an interference in your life, but **part** of it

4. Try the shot **from the hip**

5. Approach the objects of your lomographic desire as **close** as possible

6. **Don't think** (William Firebrace)

7. Be **fast**

8. You don't have to know beforehand what you captured on film

9. Afterwards either

10. **Don't worry** about any rules

The 10 Golden Rules of Lomography

ISBN: 9783902217189

First published in 2009 by Lomographic Society International
Hollergasse 41, 1150 Vienna, Austria
www.lomography.com